THE OFFICIAL

NEWCASTLE UNITED FOOTBALL CLUB

ANNUAL 2007

A Grange Publication

© 2006. Published by Grange Communications Ltd., Edinburgh under licence from Newcastle United Football Club. Printed in the EU.

Every effort has been made to ensure the accuracy of information within this publication but the publishers cannot be held responsible for any errors or omissions. Views expressed are those of the author and do not necessarily represent those of the publishers or the football club. All rights reserved.

Written by Mark Hannen. Assisted by Adam Page.

Photographs © Action Images

ISBN 0 9550057 4 4

£6.99

adidas
northern
rock

CONTENTS

NEWCASTLE UNITED
St. James' Park

GLENN ROEDER
WELCOME

Welcome to the 2007 Newcastle United FC Annual.

I am delighted to be writing this introduction as the new Manager of Newcastle United Football Club and would like to thank you all for your support during my transition from Caretaker Manager to my new role.

The feeling when I was offered the full time job was one of sheer joy and I can assure you that I, along with the players, am relishing the prospect of the 2006/07 season. Being an ex-player and captain of Newcastle United I know just what this club means to the fans and we can achieve success in the near future.

When I took over as Caretaker Manager last season we were at the wrong end of the Premiership table. However, in the 17 games that followed we gave it a really good push winning 11 and drawing 2 as well as getting to the quarter final stages of the FA Cup.

This new season is a fresh start, not least because of the retirement of Alan Shearer, although he will still be part of the club in an ambassadorial role. He did of course become our leading goalscorer before his retirement which was a fantastic achievement and his testimonial night was one that will be remembered by one and all.

That's all in the past though so now it's just a case of me saying enjoy the annual, and here's to a successful 2006/7 season.

Glenn Roeder

Farewell **Alan Shearer**

Newcastle United's newly crowned all time leading scorer called time on a fantastic career, including a magnificent decade at St James' Park, with a sold out Testimonial match on 11 May 2006.

Alan Shearer, whose final goals tally for United reached 206, was unable to play in the match due to an injury sustained at Sunderland. However, this did not matter to the 52,275 fans inside St James' Park who watched a Newcastle United team, featuring stars past and present, take on Glasgow Celtic with the number nine hero kicking off the match and coming back on to score a late penalty to win the game!

A truly memorable night drew to a close with 'Big Al' taking a final lap of honour around the pitch as the fanatical scarf-waving, Shearer-chanting crowd saw their hero in the black and white stripes for the last time.

After the match, which ended 3-2 to Newcastle, Shearer said,

"This will stay with me forever. "It has been such a special night, it has been hard and quite emotional but it has been great. I thank the fans for everything they have given me, it has been absolutely brilliant. I have had great times. I have lived my dream and done what I always wanted to do. When I was a young boy, I wanted to play for Newcastle and I have done that, it has been an incredible rollercoaster, a dream."

It was certainly a dream come true for Newcastle United fans when in 1996, the world record transfer fee was smashed to bring Shearer back home to the North East from Blackburn where he had won the Premiership title two years earlier. After a terrific display at Euro 96 where he was top scorer, there was a host of top clubs determined to get Alan to sign for them, Manchester United being one.
However there was only one club that could offer him the chance to pull on the famous number nine shirt and play in front of his own people. And so it happened. Shearer signed for the Magpies for a staggering £15m.

The crowds that gathered at St James' Park to witness the unveiling of Alan Shearer showed what a massive signing this was for the club. The fans recognised him as one of them – a Geordie with a love for Newcastle United Football Club!

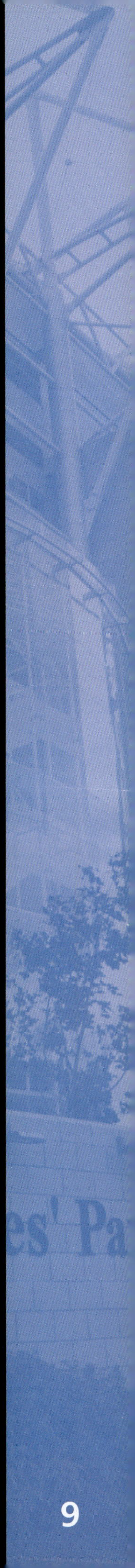

It didn't take Alan long to find the net for United. In his second league game, at home to Wimbledon, he opened his account with a splendid free kick in front of the Toon Army who would see Shearer's right hand goal celebration many times after that.

Over the next 10 years there would be many high points for the United skipper such as helping Newcastle to reach Wembley Cup Finals, a UEFA Cup Semi Final and of course breaking Jackie Milburn's scoring record. There were lows too including the defeats in the two FA Cup Finals and a couple of injuries that threatened to bring an end to Shearer's career altogether.

However, through sheer determination and a desire to give everything for his club, Alan battled on and came through these dark moments to do what he does best – score goals.

At the end of January 2006 United took on Mansfield in the 4th Round of the FA Cup and the crowd, knowing Alan was on 199 goals, held its breath to see if the skipper could do what everyone was willing him to do and equal the record. Of course he did and a week later he broke it altogether with a strike against Portsmouth to take place as Newcastle's all time leading scorer.

If the Portsmouth game was ecstasy then the Wear-Tyne derby two months later was both ecstasy and agony. Barely five minutes after scoring a penalty to claim his 206th goal and help United to a 4-1 win over Sunderland, Alan fell awkwardly under a challenge, badly damaging his knee and forcing his premature retirement from the game.

Although Alan's playing days are over he is still a huge part of Newcastle United and always will be. His new role as Sporting Ambassador will ensure his links with the club remain and the tremendous contribution he has made will never be forgotten.

Who knows what's next around the corner for the sheet metal worker's son from Gosforth.

Premier League **Season Review**

AUGUST

It was a worrying start for Newcastle United with neither a league goal nor a win throughout the first month of the season. The first match was an away trip to Highbury to face an Arsenal side playing their final season at the famous ground before moving into their newly built stadium.

A first class display by United was hampered by the harsh sending off of Jermaine Jenas. However Newcastle clung on, more than matching Arsenal, until Thierry Henry clinically dispatched a penalty before Robin Van Persie doubled the lead at the death.

Newly promoted West Ham United were the first league visitors to St James' Park but despite a few efforts on goal, Newcastle could not break the deadlock even when the sending off of Paul Konchesksy reduced West Ham to 10 men.

ARSENAL 2	**NEWCASTLE** 0
NEWCASTLE 0	**WEST HAM UNITED** 0
BOLTON WANDERERS 2	**NEWCASTLE** 0
NEWCASTLE 0	**MANCHESTER UNITED** 2

The goal drought continued with a trip to the Reebok Stadium to face a Bolton side who had qualified for Europe for the first time in their history. Goals either side of half time, the second looking to be offside, saw Bolton take a 2-0 lead and only a headed clearance off the line by Stephen Carr spared a third.

Manchester United were the next visitors to St James' Park but injuries to Kieron Dyer, Emre and Lee Bowyer turned the game and Manchester United were quick to capitalise with Wayne Rooney and Ruud Van Nistelrooy grabbing a goal each.

SEPTEMBER

In a week of high activity in the transfer market the Toon Army got the news they had all been waiting for – Michael Owen had signed for the Magpies.

The former Liverpool and Real Madrid star was thrust straight back into Premiership action for the visit of Fulham. After going a goal down early on, it looked like the Magpies would be facing another defeat until a superb free kick by Charles N'Zogbia levelled things.

Graeme Souness' former club Blackburn Rovers were up next as Newcastle travelled to Ewood Park still searching for their first win of the season. And they did it in spectacular style. Alan Shearer nearly broke the net with his shot into the right hand corner before Michael Owen opened his account with a near post header. Charles N'Zogbia wrapped things up with a cheeky roll over with his left foot to leave Brad Friedel helpless.

Newcastle were on the hunt for another win, this time at home to Manchester City. A single goal did it and it was record signing Michael Owen who provided it, scoring his first goal at St James' Park for The Magpies.

NEWCASTLE 1 (N'Zogbia)	**FULHAM** 1
BLACKBURN ROVERS 0	**NEWCASTLE** 3 (Shearer, Owen, N'Zogbia)
NEWCASTLE 1 (Owen)	**MANCHESTER CITY** 0

OCTOBER

Newcastle United had never managed a win against Portsmouth at Fratton Park in the Premiership and unfortunately that was not to change on this occasion.

It could easily have been a defeat though and only some fantastic saves from Shay Given preserved a point for the Magpies.

Next up it was off to the JJB Stadium for the first time to face Premiership debutants Wigan Athletic. Unfortunately United's luck ran out once again when, already chasing the game after going a goal down, an Alan Shearer header which blatantly crossed the line before being cleared was disallowed by referee Phil Dowd.

Sunderland's promotion to the Premiership meant the North East derby games made a welcome return. A crowd of 52,302 turned out to see the 127th league meeting between the two teams and they were treated to a match full of goals.

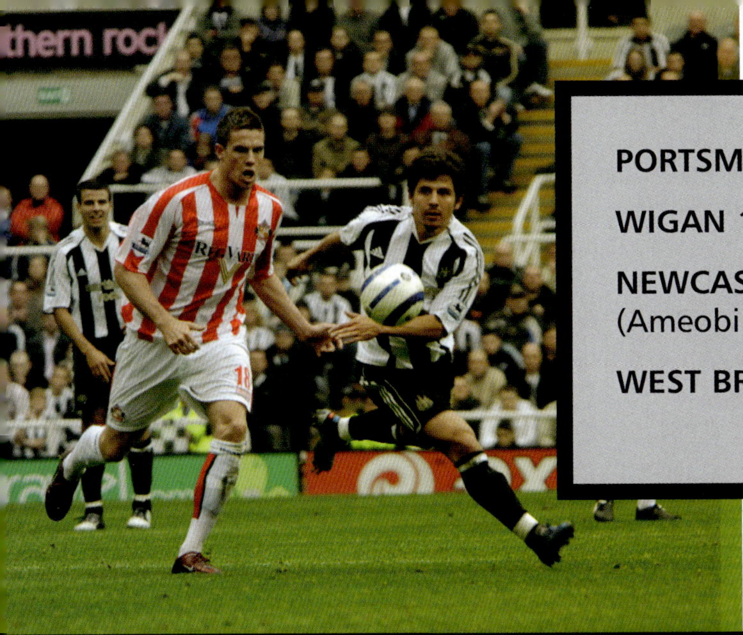

PORTSMOUTH 0	**NEWCASTLE** 0
WIGAN 1	**NEWCASTLE** 0
NEWCASTLE 3 (Ameobi 2, Emre)	**SUNDERLAND** 2
WEST BROMWICH ALBION 0	**NEWCASTLE** 3 (Owen 2, Shearer)

A period of eight minutes in the first half saw Newcastle go ahead twice through Shola Ameobi headers, only for Sunderland to reply almost immediately. The scores stayed level until a superb Emre free kick from 25 yards settled things.

Having shrugged off their early season problem of not scoring, Newcastle travelled to face West Bromwich Albion and duly won the game 3 – 0. It took Michael Owen just 23 seconds into the second half to find the net with a superb volley. He followed it up with another strike before Alan Shearer hit the third.

NOVEMBER

Birmingham were next up at St James' Park and although the Blues did force Newcastle to battle and grind out a result, it was Turkish midfielder Emre who provided the solitary goal in the form of a 20 yard shot that City goalkeeper Maik Taylor failed to deal with.

Having never registered a win in the Premiership at Stamford Bridge, playing Chelsea away had become a miserable trip for the fans and this next fixture turned out to be no different. United started brightly, but second half goals from Joe Cole, Hernan Crespo and Damien Duff saw United off.

NEWCASTLE 1 (Emre)	**BIRMINGHAM CITY** 0
CHELSEA 3	**NEWCASTLE** 0
EVERTON 1	**NEWCASTLE** 0

Newcastle remained on their travels the following week, playing Everton at Goodison Park. Two efforts from Alan Shearer could have seen the Magpies take the lead, and after United were denied a clear penalty, Joseph Yobo headed the only goal of the game.

DECEMBER

It was a rare penalty, and some even rarer good fortune that saw Newcastle earn a point against Aston Villa. Alan Shearer fired home United's first penalty of the season before Gavin McCann equalised but as full time approached, the visitors missed out on all three points when Gareth Barry sent his penalty kick high over the bar.

After being robbed of a result at Highbury, United were looking for revenge when Arsenal visited St James' Park. A battling display saw United take all three points thanks to a Nobby Solano goal and excellent performances by Peter Ramage and Scott Parker.

Newcastle's final fixture before the Christmas period, and a hectic schedule of games, was away to West Ham United and it brought Michael Owen's first Newcastle hat-trick, as well as Alan Shearer's 199th goal for United.

NEWCASTLE 1 (Shearer pen)	**ASTON VILLA** 1
NEWCASTLE 1 (Solano)	**ARSENAL** 0
WEST HAM UNITED 2	**NEWCASTLE** 4 (Owen 3, Shearer)
LIVERPOOL 2	**NEWCASTLE** 0
TOTTENHAM HOTSPUR 2	**NEWCASTLE** 0

Boxing Day at Anfield brought no joy where Steven Gerrard and Peter Crouch scored for the home side. Sadly, Steven Taylor, making his comeback after injury, suffered another dislocation of his right shoulder.

United were at White Hart Lane on New Year's Eve, and aside from the 2 – 0 defeat, it will be remembered for Michael Owen breaking his fifth metatarsal. 2005 certainly didn't finish kindly for United.

JANUARY

The first match of 2006 was a Tyne-Tees derby with Middlesbrough. United took the lead with an excellent Nobby Solano free kick and after Boro hit back with two goals it was Geordie boy Lee Clark who salvaged a point for the Magpies in injury time. United's visit to Craven Cottage brought a miserable 1 – 0 defeat leaving the Magpies in a lowly 13th position, a consequence of their disappointing away form.

The return of Graeme Souness' former club Blackburn Rovers was to bring yet more misfortune for United, Morten Gamst Pedersen claiming the winning goal with what looked like a clear handball.

NEWCASTLE 2 (Solano, Clark)	**MIDDLESBROUGH** 2
FULHAM 1	**NEWCASTLE** 0
NEWCASTLE 0	**BLACKBURN** 1

FEBRUARY

United's next fixture, a midweek trip to face Manchester City, was to be Graeme Souness' last as Newcastle manager. Having only one shot on target at a freezing Eastlands stadium told its own story and the Magpies were soundly beaten 3-0.

Souness' replacement was to be found close to home in the form of Newcastle United Academy Manager Glenn Roeder, an ex-player, and captain, of United in the 1980s.

Roeder took on the role of caretaker manager and he was in the dugout for the visit of Portsmouth. Charles N'Zogbia tucked away his fourth goal of the season just before the break but it was in the 63rd minute that St James' Park erupted. Shola Ameobi held the ball up towards the Pompey goal and his well timed back heel was enough to send the ball into Shearer's path to slot it past the advancing Dean Kiely. Goal number 201 was secured.

With the record broken and Newcastle United playing with renewed belief, Aston Villa were the next team to feel the force of the Geordie resurgence with United winning 2 – 1 at Villa Park.

The rescheduled game against Charlton Athletic turned out to be an uneventful encounter. Neither side could break the deadlock and the final whistle was a welcome relief for those inside a bitterly cold St James' Park.

A resurgent Everton were next on Tyneside in a game notable for one of United's goals of the season, a wonderful curling shot from Nobby Solano was his second of the game and it sent the Toffees home pointless.

MANCHESTER CITY 3	**NEWCASTLE** 0
NEWCASTLE 2 (N'Zogbia, Shearer)	**PORTSMOUTH** 0
ASTON VILLA 1	**NEWCASTLE** 2 (Ameobi, N'Zogbia)
NEWCASTLE 0	**CHARLTON ATHLETIC** 0
NEWCASTLE 2 (Solano 2)	**EVERTON** 0

MARCH

Newcastle started March looking to maintain their unbeaten run since the arrival of Glenn Roeder and duly did so against a Bolton side with goals from Nobby Solano, Alan Shearer and Shola Ameobi. Whilst the Newcastle revival was evident, a tricky away encounter at Old Trafford loomed next.

Manchester United, and in particular Wayne Rooney, were a formidable force and the game was effectively over after 15 minutes, Wayne Rooney having netted twice.

NEWCASTLE 3 (Solano, Shearer, Ameobi)	**BOLTON WANDERERS 1**
MANCHESTER UNITED 2	**NEWCASTLE 0**
NEWCASTLE 1 (Ameobi)	**LIVERPOOL 3**
CHARLTON ATHLETIC 3	**NEWCASTLE 1** (Parker)

The fixture list did not get any easier with Liverpool the visitors at St James' Park the following week. Two goals in the first half from Peter Crouch and the inspirational Steven Gerrard meant things were looking bad for United and when Djibril Cisse tucked away the third from the penalty spot after the break, the game was as good as over.

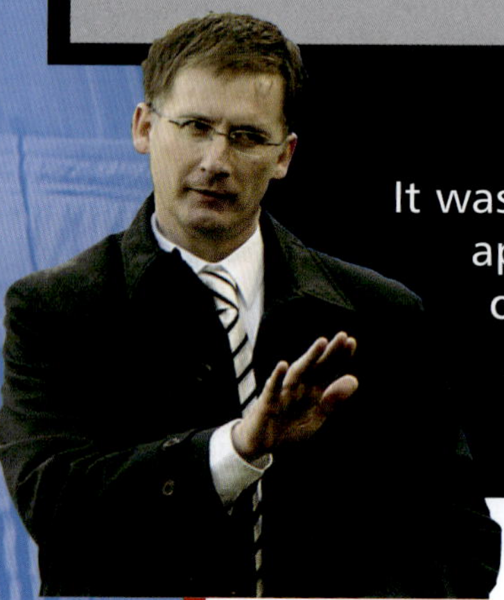

It was on to the Valley next where Scott Parker, making his last appearance of the season due to a bout of glandular fever, signed off in style with a spectacular 25 yard goal. Three goals for the Addicks though put an end to Parker's and United's celebrations.

APRIL

Thankfully the Charlton game was to be the last time Newcastle would taste defeat in 2005/06. United were on fire against Tottenham and after opening the scoring in only the second minute they never looked back and eased to a comfortable victory.

With this victory came renewed optimism with European qualification still possible. The Tees-Tyne derby was to be the scene of United's next climb up the Premiership table, the Magpies grabbing an excellent away win on Teesside.

Wigan were the next side to be despatched at St. James' Park, with United coming from behind to claim victory, the first time they had done so in nearly two years.

NEWCASTLE 3 (Bowyer, Ameobi, Shearer pen)	**TOTTENHAM HOTSPUR** 1
MIDDLESBROUGH 1	**NEWCASTLE** 2 (Boateng og, Ameobi)
NEWCASTLE 3 (Shearer 2 (1 pen), Bramble)	**WIGAN ATHLETIC** 1
SUNDERLAND 1	**NEWCASTLE** 4 (Chopra, Shearer pen, N'Zogbia, Luque)
NEWCASTLE 3 (Solano, Ameobi 2 (1 pen))	**WEST BROMWICH ALBION** 0
BIRMINGHAM CITY 0	**NEWCASTLE** 0

The next fixture, the Wear-Tyne derby, looked certain to be the last for at least another year with Sunderland's impending relegation, however it was hard to tell who were the struggling team in the first half with Newcastle a goal down at the break after a poor display. But four dramatic second half goals, including Alan Shearer's last ever goal for United made it a jubilant away day for United.

Spirits were dampened though when Alan Shearer, under a challenge from Julio Arca, went down with a knee injury which forced the skipper to be taken off and make this appearance his last for Newcastle.

The penultimate home game of the season saw relegation-bound West Bromwich Albion visit St James' Park. This game, a 3 – 0 win, saw 19 year old Matty Pattison make his full league debut and he acquitted himself extremely well.

Newcastle faced another team destined for the Coca Cola Championship the following week. Birmingham put up more resistance than their Midlands neighbours WBA, the game finishing scoreless but the point was not enough to save the Blues from relegation.

MAY

With Newcastle sitting in seventh place and contesting a place in the Intertoto Cup with Bolton Wanderers, the final game of the season against Chelsea was no meaningless match with nothing to play for.

A fantastic performance from Newcastle made for a thrilling atmosphere inside St James' Park and highlighted just how much was at stake in this match. Bolton had taken the lead in their game so it was vital United took all three points. And this they did through an explosive volley from Titus Bramble which confirmed seventh place and the all important entry into the Intertoto Cup.

NEWCASTLE 1 (Bramble)	**CHELSEA** 0

A truly miraculous turnaround had been achieved and Glenn Roeder was rewarded for his work when he was made Newcastle United's permanent manager a week later.

QUIZ

What do you remember about the 2005/06 season?

1 Who scored United's first Premiership goal of the season?

2 Who knocked United out of the Intertoto Cup?

3 Which team did United sign Emre from?

4 Against which team did Michael Owen score his only home goal?

5 Against which team did Alan Shearer equal Jackie Milburn's United goals record?

6 Which United player transferred to Tottenham in August 2005?

7 Who equalised for United in the last minute against Middlesbrough at St. James' Park?

8 Blackburn, Man Utd, and which other team were the only away teams to win at Newcastle in 2005/06?

9 Who was Glenn Roeder's first game as caretaker manager against?

10 Against which team did Michael Owen break his metatarsal?

Answers on page 61

SEASON STATISTICS 2005/06

NAME	APPEARANCES AND GOALS				
	League	FA Cup	Lge Cup	Europe	Total
Shola AMEOBI	25 (5) 9	3 (0) 0	0 (0) 0	0 (1) 0	28 (6) 9
Celestine BABAYARO	26 (2) 0	3 (0) 0	1 (0) 0	3 (0) 0	33 (2) 0
Lee BOWYER	18 (10) 1	1 (1) 0	1 (0) 0	3 (0) 1	23 (11) 2
Jean Alain BOUMSONG	30 (3) 0	3 (0) 0	1 (0) 0	4 (0) 0	38 (3) 0
Titus BRAMBLE	21 (3) 2	3 (0) 0	1 (0) 0	0 (0) 0	25 (3) 2
Stephen CARR	19 (0) 0	2 (0) 0	0 (0) 0	3 (0) 0	24 (0) 0
Michael CHOPRA	6 (7) 1	1 (1) 1	1 (1) 0	1 (2) 1	9 (11) 3
Lee CLARK	8 (14) 1	2 (0) 0	0 (1) 0	0 (0) 0	10 (15) 1
Kieron DYER	4 (7) 0	2 (0) 1	0 (0) 0	0 (0) 0	6 (7) 1
Robbie ELLIOTT	14 (3) 0	2 (0) 0	1 (0) 0	2 (0) 0	19 (3) 0
EMRE	19 (1) 2	1 (2) 0	1 (0) 0	1 (0) 0	22 (3) 2
Amady FAYE	14 (8) 0	0 (0) 0	1 (1) 0	4 (0) 0	19 (9) 0
Shay GIVEN	38 (0) 0	4 (0) 0	2 (0) 0	3 (0) 0	47 (0) 0
Steve HARPER	0 (0) 0	0 (0) 0	0 (0) 0	1 (0) 0	1 (0) 0
Albert LUQUE	6 (8) 1	1 (2) 0	1 (0) 0	0 (0) 0	8 (10) 1
Craig MOORE	8 (0) 0	0 (1) 0	0 (0) 0	0 (0) 0	8 (1) 0
Charles N'ZOGBIA	27 (5) 5	2 (1) 0	2 (0) 0	3 (1) 1	34 (7) 6
Alan O'BRIEN	0 (3) 0	0 (1) 0	0 (0) 0	0 (0) 0	0 (4) 0
Michael OWEN	10 (1) 7	0 (0) 0	0 (0) 0	0 (0) 0	10 (1) 7
Scott PARKER	26 (0) 1	3 (0) 1	2 (0) 0	1 (0) 0	32 (0) 2
Matthew PATTISON	2 (1) 0	0 (0) 0	0 (0) 0	0 (0) 0	2 (1) 0
Peter RAMAGE	23 (0) 0	3 (1) 0	2 (0) 0	0 (0) 0	28 (1) 0
Alan SHEARER	31 (1) 10	3 (0) 1	2 (0) 1	4 (0) 2	40 (1) 14
Nobby SOLANO	27 (2) 6	4 (0) 0	2 (0) 0	0 (0) 0	33 (2) 6
Steven TAYLOR	12 (0) 0	0 (0) 0	1 (0) 0	4 (0) 0	17 (0) 0

HALF TIME RECORD 2005/06 (PREMIERSHIP ONLY)

FIRST HALF RECORD
Played 38– Won 11 – Drawn 17 – Lost 10

SECOND HALF RECORD
Played 38 – Won 13 – Drawn 11 – Lost 14

FIRST HALF GOALS
Goals scored 23 – Goals against 21

SECOND HALF GOALS
Goals scored 24 – Goals against 21

SCORED FIRST

Played	38
Newcastle United score first	17
Opponents score first	17
No goals scored	4
Newcastle United score first & win	15
Newcastle United score first & draw	2
Newcastle United score first & lose	0
Opponents score first & win	14
Opponents score first & draw	1
Opponents score first & lose	2
Newcastle United fail to score	16
Opponents fail to score	13

UNITED'S GOALSCORING RECORDS 2005/06 (PREMIERSHIP)

BIGGEST HOME WIN	Newcastle 3 – 0 West Brom (22 April 2006)
WORST HOME DEFEAT	Newcastle 1 – 3 Liverpool (19 March 2006)
BIGGEST AWAY WIN	Sunderland 1 – 4 Newcastle (17 April 2006)
WORST AWAY DEFEAT	Chelsea 3 – 0 Newcastle (19 November 2005)
	Man City 3 – 0 Newcastle (1 February 2006)

AVERAGE HOME ATTENDANCE:	52,032
AVERAGE AWAY ATTENDANCE:	34,043

HIGHEST (H):	52,327 v Manchester United (28 August 2005)
HIGHEST (A):	67,858 v Manchester United (12 March 2006)
LOWEST (H):	50,451 v Charlton (22 February 2006)
LOWEST (A):	20,220 v Portsmouth (1 October 2005)

GOALS SCORED BY GAME

0 GOALS	16
1 GOAL	8
2 GOALS	5
3 GOALS	7
4 GOALS	2
5 GOALS	0

GOALS CONCEDED BY GAME

0 GOALS	13
1 GOAL	12
2 GOALS	9
3 GOALS	4
4 GOALS	0
5 GOALS	0

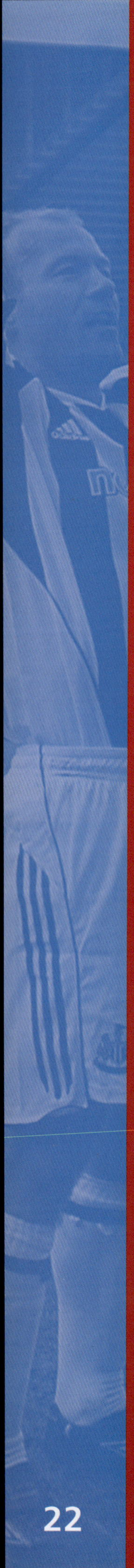

FA CUP REVIEW

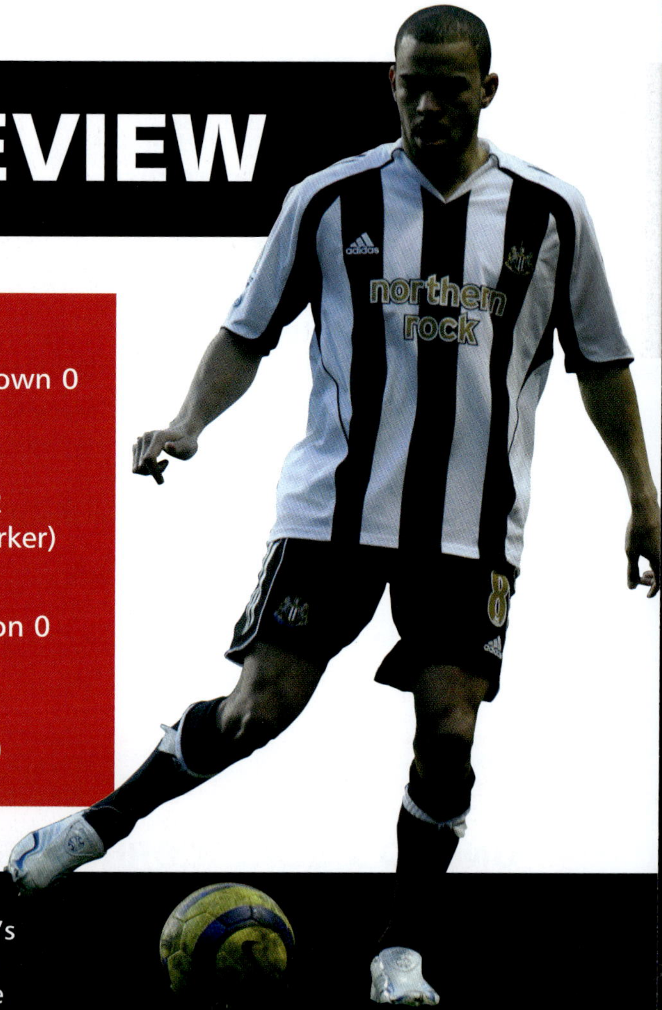

RESULTS

3RD ROUND

Newcastle 1 (Shearer)	Mansfield Town 0

4TH ROUND

Cheltenham Town 0	Newcastle 2 (Chopra, Parker)

5TH ROUND

Newcastle 1 (Dyer)	Southampton 0

QUARTER FINAL

Chelsea 1	Newcastle 0

The New Year brought with it Newcastle's involvement in the FA Cup and the Toon Army hoped that success could finally be on its way to St James' Park after reaching the semi-finals the previous year.

In Round Three Newcastle left it late against Mansfield Town to take the lead and guarantee a place in the next round. The goal that took United through was Alan Shearer's 200th for the club, putting him alongside Jackie Milburn as Newcastle's all time leading scorer.

A trip to face Cheltenham Town came in Round Four and facing a side determined to create another FA Cup 'giant killing', Newcastle had a challenging afternoon ahead.

The first half saw penalty appeals waved away from both sides but five minutes before half time a Celestine Babayaro cross, hitting Cheltenham goalkeeper Shane Higgs, was headed into the back of the net by Michael Chopra to claim his first domestic goal for United. The tie was all over for Cheltenham two minutes later when an attempted clearance by defender Jerry Gill rebounded off the chest of Scott Parker and into the Cheltenham goal.

Unavailable through injury, Alan Shearer was not able to face his old club one last time when Southampton visited St James' Park in Round Five. The breakthrough came when Kieron Dyer, sent through by Charles N'Zogbia, went on a blistering run past the Southampton defence before sending the ball into the back of the net.

The draw for the next round, undertaken by former Magpie Rob Lee, gave Newcastle a daunting trip to London to face Premiership Champions Chelsea.

The home side took the lead on four minutes through John Terry and with a mountain to climb Newcastle put in a determined performance and had the opportunity to equalise when Carlo Cudicini was forced to parry a shot, only for Alan Shearer to be beaten to the ball by Terry. This seemed to sum up United's night and meant the long wait for silverware was set to last for at least another season.

LEAGUE CUP REVIEW

RESULTS

3RD ROUND
Grimsby Town 0 Newcastle 1
(Shearer)

4TH ROUND
Wigan Athletic 1 Newcastle 0

Newcastle United's record in the League Cup over recent years has not been the most impressive having never got further than the Quarter Final stages since their only Cup Final appearance back in 1976 - unfortunately 2005/6 was not to be 'the year' either.

United's first tie saw them up against League Two side Grimsby Town at Blundell Park. This was United's first visit to the home of the Mariners since they clinched the First Division title there in the 1992/93 season.

A crowd of 9,311 turned out on a wet night in anticipation of another upset after Grimsby had dumped Tottenham Hotspur out of the Cup in the previous round. However it was Alan Shearer who was the difference between the two sides. With only 10 minutes remaining, strike partner Michael Chopra picked up the ball on the right and threaded it through to Shearer who blasted home with his left foot.

Newcastle were through and the midweek draw handed them another away fixture in Round Four, this time to recently promoted Wigan Athletic.

Newcastle were overwhelmed by an under strength Wigan side as early as the second minute and if not for some incredible saves by Shay Given, the Magpies would have gone into the break at least a couple of goals down.

The goal did come Wigan's way, and although it came in the form of a cruel late penalty, after Robbie Elliott fouled Jason Roberts, Newcastle could have no complaints after what was a sub standard performance. As for Wigan, they went all the way to Cardiff for the Final.

MICHAEL OWEN

Michael Owen's arrival on Tyneside stunned the football world. Here was a genuine world superstar transferring from one of the most famous clubs in the world, Real Madrid, to Newcastle United.

Naturally many of Europe's top clubs were linked with his signature but United beat them all to it and the player, who marked his entrance onto the world stage with a quite outstanding solo effort against Argentina in the 1998 World Cup, became Newcastle United's record signing. It was a magical day for everyone connected with the Club.

And what a welcome he received on a sunny Tuesday afternoon at the end of August as an adoring Tyneside public turned up in their thousands to greet the latest in a long line of adopted Geordie heroes. There were scenes of incredible emotion as he strode out on to the St. James' Park pitch for the first time in a black and white shirt.

Unfortunately for Michael, injuries played a huge part in making his first season at Newcastle a disappointing one, but when he did play, he delivered goals by the plateful. Seven goals in 10 Premiership games for the Magpies was some start but the cruel foot injury suffered at Tottenham on New Year's Eve, was a devastating blow to all of Tyneside, not least to the player himself.

The Michael Owen story began in professional football when the Chester born striker made his debut, and scored, aged 17, for Liverpool at Wimbledon in the penultimate game of the 1996/97 season. He went on to make 267 starts for The Reds in all competitions, with a further 30 from the bench, and netted an impressive 158 goals. Off the pitch he collected the PFA Young Player of the Year for season 1997-98 and in 1998 was also voted BBC Sports Personality of the Year.

It was in the treble season of 2000/01 that Owen continued and enhanced his reputation, scoring two magnificent late goals to win the FA Cup Final for Liverpool in Cardiff against Arsenal. Michael was named European Footballer of the Year in December 2001 when he received the prestigious 'ballon D'or'.

In the 2002/03 season Owen scored 28 goals for Liverpool including his 100th in the Premiership, he also scored at the Millennium Stadium in Cardiff again when Liverpool beat Manchester United 2-0 to win the Worthington Cup. Michael left Anfield for Real Madrid in August 2004, and made 20 starts for the Spanish giants, and a further 15 from the bench, netting 13 La Liga goals.

Owen has been capped 80 times for his country, and his 36 goals see him positioned fourth in the all-time England hotshots list behind Bobby Charlton (49), Gary Lineker (48) and Jimmy Greaves (44). His hat-trick against Germany in Munich in September 2001, as England beat their hosts 5-1 to ensure qualification for the 2002 World Cup, demonstrated his phenomenal scoring prowess and he hit his second international hat-trick in England's 3 – 2 win against Colombia in May 2005. Michael's goal against Poland on 12 October 2005, his 33rd for England, equalled Gary Lineker's tally of competitive goals for his country (22).

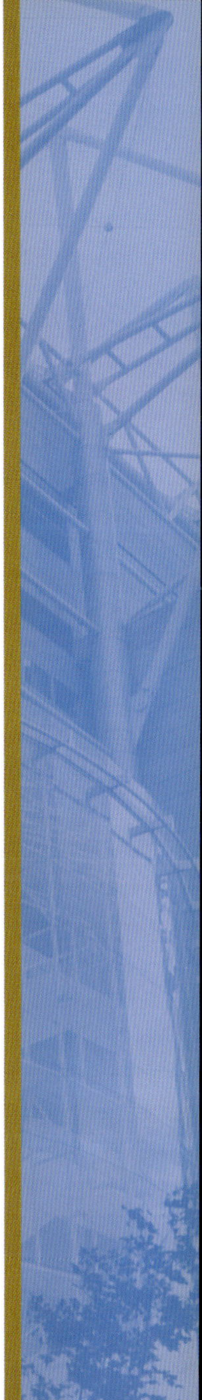

CLUB HONOURS

2001 Golden Boot (European Footballer of the Year)
2001 European SuperCup winner
2001 UEFA Cup winner
2001 FA Cup winner
2001 Charity Shield winner
2003 League Cup winner

ALL-TIME GREATS

Defining who is a Newcastle United great is a thankless task. So here we have just concentrated on the post war years, which discounts the likes of Jimmy Lawrence, Bill McCracken and Colin Veitch, and picked 10 players who have worn the black and white shirt with distinction. And to keep the historical theme, we've not included any players from this decade.

IVOR ALLCHURCH (1958 - 1962)

Ivor was one of the finest attacking midfielders to appear in post war football. Born in Swansea, Ivor joined United from the Swans and scored 51 goals in 154 games for the Magpies. Ivor, who won 68 Wales caps had tremendous ability and played with great panache and possessed bundles of skill. Not only that but he had tremendous shooting ability and was deceptively quick. A magnificent footballer who would certainly grace the modern game.

PETER BEARDSLEY (1983 - 87 & 1993 - 97)

A true United legend, Peter appeared for the Magpies in two separate spells, first with the likes of Kevin Keegan and Chris Waddle in the mid 1980s, and then under Keegan the Manager. Peter is recognised by many as the best player to have pulled on the black and white shirt. Slight of build but possessing fantastic ball skills and marvellous vision. The holder of 59 England caps, Peter scored 119 goals in 326 games for United, many of which were truly spectacular.

FRANK BRENNAN (1946 - 56)

Born in Scotland, Frank was a tremendous centre-half for Newcastle United, rated by many as the best to have played for the Magpies in over a century of football. Known as the 'Rock of Tyneside' he was cool headed, steady and tough. Frank relished a duel with the big name centre-forwards of his day and was a key player as United lifted the FA Cup in 1951 and 1952.

TONY GREEN (1971 – 73)

Although only playing 39 times for the Magpies, the all too brief Newcastle United career of Tony Green is fondly cherished by all those supporters fortunate enough to have seen him play. Brought to Tyneside by Joe Harvey from Blackpool, Tony had exceptional ability on the ball and buzzing with enthusiasm, he would dart into action jinking past players in midfield. Green was a genius but his career was tragically cut short when a knee ligament injury forced his retirement.

MALCOLM MACDONALD (1971 - 76)

A seventies icon Supermac was hero worshipped at St. James' Park for his goal scoring feats and the excitement he brought to the United supporters. Built like a middle-weight boxer, he was a brash and colourful centre-forward. Blessed with electric pace and a thunderous shot, Supermac terrorised defences scoring 138 goals for United in only 258 games. A hat-trick against Liverpool on his home debut signalled his intention and he also hit five goals in an England shirt against Cyprus in 1975.

JACKIE MILBURN (1943 - 57)

Wor Jackie held Newcastle United's goalscoring record until 2006 when Alan Shearer surpassed his tremendous feat. Born in Ashington, local boy Jackie became the archetypal Geordie hero as his goalscoring ability took Tyneside by storm. Jackie relished the big match atmosphere and created headlines over and over again with his spectacular strikes. A three time FA Cup winner with the Magpies in the 1950s Jackie, who won 13 England caps, scoring 10 goals, left an impression on everyone who saw him play, or knew him as a person.

BOBBY MITCHELL (1949 - 61)

Along with club colleagues Frank Brennan and Jackie Milburn, Bobby Mitchell was the darling of the Newcastle crowd during the immediate post war years. Known throughout football as 'Bobby Dazzler' he was famed for his immaculate ball control and wing wizardry. A three time Cup winner, Bobby thrilled the United crowd with his magic footwork and ball skills in a 13-year Gallowgate career that saw him hit the net 113 times in 410 games.

BOBBY MONCUR (1960 - 74)

Captain of United and also of Scotland, Bobby was the man who lifted the Inter Cities Fairs Cup for the Magpies back in 1969, after the black & whites beat the Hungarians Ujpest Dozsa. Remarkably, Moncur also helped himself to three goals in the Final, and considering he only scored 10 goals in total for United in 361 appearances, that was some feat. An excellent central defender, Moncur, a rugged and determined player, marshalled the United backline superbly during his 14 years on Tyneside.

CHRIS WADDLE (1980 - 85)

Chris Waddle was an immensely talented ball playing winger who helped set United alight in the early to mid 1980s. Having signed from non league Tow Law, Chris blossomed into an international class talent. With the rare ability to go past defenders using a body swerve and deceptive pace, Waddle played right across United's front line putting in dangerous crosses or hitting the target with viciously bending shots. Chris won 62 England caps and played in the 1986 and 1990 World Cups.

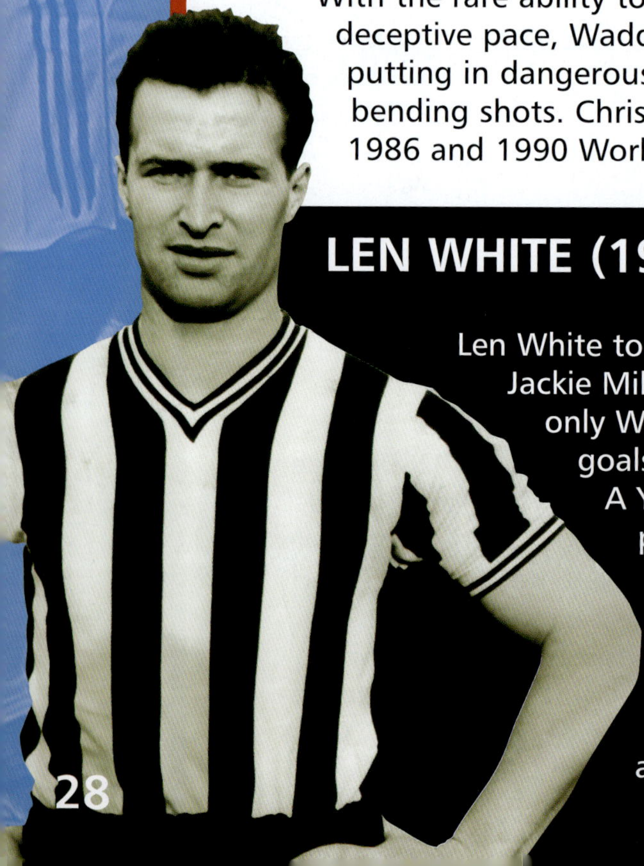

LEN WHITE (1953 - 62)

Len White took over the United goalscoring mantle from Jackie Milburn and Vic Keeble in the late 1950s and only Wor Jackie and Alan Shearer have scored more goals for the Magpies in league and cup football. A Yorkshireman, Len was of stocky build but possessed terrific strength on the ball, weaving in and out of challenges at speed and finishing with a power packed shot. Unfortunate not to win a full England cap, Len did notch a notable eight minute hat-trick playing for a Football League XI against Ireland.

QUIZ 2

See how much you know about Newcastle United past and present!

1. How many goals did Michael Owen score in his first season with the Magpies?
2. Which team did Newcastle United play against at Alan Shearer's Testimonial?
3. Which NUFC Academy player made his first league start last season?
4. In which year did Newcastle United win the Inter Cities Fairs Cup (now UEFA Cup)?
5. Which London club did Glenn Roeder manage before Newcastle?
6. In which season did the Magpies pull off the classic 5-0 win against Manchester United?
7. Which current squad member has the most number of appearances for Newcastle United?
8. Which player re-signed for Newcastle from Aston Villa in the 2005/6 season?
9. How many times have Newcastle won the FA Cup?
10. In which season did Newcastle United play their first game in the Premiership?

Answers on page 61

EUROPEAN HISTORY

Did you know that Newcastle United are one of only 13 English teams to have won a major European Trophy? For back in 1969, the Magpies won the Inter Cities Fairs Cup (now called the UEFA Cup) with an epic 6 – 2 two legged aggregate win over the Hungarians of Ujpest Dozsa.

And what's more, United success that year came during the first season they had qualified for the competition, making their triumph even more noteworthy.

Since then United have enjoyed mixed success with their forays into Europe, including a run to second group phase of the Champions League in 2002/03, and a semi final appearance in the UEFA Cup in 2003/04.

THE FULL SUMMARY OF EUROPEAN CAMPAIGNS IS:

1968/69 - Inter Cities Fairs Cup	Winners
1969/70 - Inter Cities Fairs Cup	Quarter Final
1970/71 - Inter Cities Fairs Cup	Round Two
1977/78 - UEFA Cup	Round Two
1994/95 - UEFA Cup	Round Two
1996/97 - UEFA Cup	Quarter Final
1997/98 - Champions League	First Group Phase
1998/99 - Cup Winners Cup	Round One
1999/00 - UEFA Cup	Round Three
2001/02 - Intertoto Cup	Did not qualify for UEFA Cup
2002/03 - Champions League	Second Group Phase
2003/04 - Champions League	Qualifying round
- UEFA Cup	Semi Finalists
2004/05 - UEFA Cup	Quarter Final
2005/06 - Intertoto Cup	Did not qualify for UEFA Cup

UNITED'S COMPLETE RECORD

	Pl	W	D	L	F	A
Home	53	39	6	8	112	42
Away	53	20	13	20	76	69
Total	**106**	**59**	**19**	**28**	**188**	**111**

MISCELLANEOUS RECORDS

Biggest Home Win	Newcastle 5 – 0 NEC Breda (UEFA Cup 2003/04)
Biggest Away Win	Antwerp 0 – 5 Newcastle (UEFA Cup 1994/95)
Worst Home Defeat	Newcastle 1 – 4 Inter Milan (Champions League 2002/03)
Worst Away Defeat	Monaco 3 – 0 Newcastle (UEFA Cup 1996/97)
	Sporting Lisbon 4 – 1 Newcastle (UEFA Cup 2004/05)
Highest Home Attendance	59,309, Newcastle v Anderlecht (Fairs Cup 1969/70)
Highest Away Attendance	98,000, Dynamo Kiev v Newcastle (Champions League 1997/98)

EUROPEAN APPEARANCES

(TOP 6)

1	Shay Given	54
2	Alan Shearer	49
3	Aaron Hughes	44
4	Gary Speed	39
5	Andy O'Brien	37
6	Shola Ameobi	37

EUROPEAN GOAL SCORERS

(TOP 6)

1	Alan Shearer	30
2	Craig Bellamy	11
3	Shola Ameobi	10
4	Wyn Davies	10
5	Bryan Robson	9
6	Tino Asprilla	9

WHERE IN THE WORLD?

There was a time when United's players were mainly English, with a few Scottish and Welsh players thrown in. Nowadays the Premiership is a global industry and the Magpies squad of 2006/07 hails from many different countries and environments. Below is a map showing exactly where in the world some of the players have come from to play their football in Newcastle.

STEPHEN CARR
DUBLIN,
IRELAND
CHARLES
N'ZOGBIA
HARFLEUR,
FRANCE
EMRE
ISTANBUL,
TURKEY
CELESTINE
BABAYARO
KADUNA,
NIGERIA
JEAN ALAIN
BOUMSONG
DOUALA,
CAMEROON
CRAIG MOORE
CANTERBURY,
AUSTRALIA

SHOLA AMEOBI - 23

BORN
12 October 1981, Zaria, Nigeria
POSITION
Striker
DEBUT
9 September 2000 v Chelsea (H)
PREVIOUS CLUBS
None

Talented striker with a penchant for the unpredictable. Born in Nigeria, Shola came to England with his parents at the age of five and is a product of the Newcastle United Academy. He further demonstrated his potential with a well taken goal and terrific all round display against Barcelona in the Champions League in the Nou Camp in December 2002. A brace in the Tyne/Wear derby on 23 October 2005 helped earn United their 4th successive derby victory. Made his 200th United appearance at Charlton on 26 March 2006.

CELESTINE BABAYARO - 33

BORN	29 August 1978, Kaduna, Nigeria
POSITION	Left Back
DEBUT	9 January 2005 v Yeading (A)
PREVIOUS CLUBS	Anderlecht, Chelsea

Nigerian international left back Celestine Babayaro joined the Magpies from Chelsea. Babayaro shot to fame with a series of glittering performances for Nigeria in the 1996 Olympic Games in Atlanta, he then moved to Chelsea in 1997 having spent his career up until then with Anderlecht where he made his debut aged only 16. An excellent defender who reads the game well, Babayaro played in the 1998 and 2002 World Cup Finals and last season he played a major part in United's successful late season run under Glenn Roeder.

EMRE BELOZOGLU - 5

BORN	7 September 1980, Istanbul, Turkey
POSITION	Midfield
DEBUT	3 August 2005 v Deportivo (H)
PREVIOUS CLUBS	Galatasaray, Inter Milan

Emre Belözoglu joined United in July 2005, being one of the most highly talented Turkish football players of all time and was instrumental in Galatasaray's UEFA Cup victory in 2000, and Turkey's impressive third-place finish in the 2002 World Cup. Emre, an attacking left sided midfielder, joined United from Italian giants Internazionale and immediately became a crowd favourite at St. James' Park. He hit the winner, and his first United goal, a stunning free kick, in the 3-2 derby win over Sunderland on 23 October 2005.

JEAN ALAIN BOUMSONG - 6

BORN	14 December 1979, Douala, Cameroon
POSITION	Centre Half
DEBUT	9 January 2005 v Yeading (A)
PREVIOUS CLUBS	Le Havre, Auxerre, Rangers

Boumsong, well built and with good pace, joined the Magpies from Glasgow Rangers. Born in Douala, Cameroon, he moved to France, eventually joining Auxerre. Being part of the French squad at Euro 2004, Boumsong's fine form had attracted the attention of Glasgow Rangers and he signed for the Ibrox side in June 2004. Jean Alain became the 12th Frenchman to wear the black and white shirt of United in the Premiership, the first being David Ginola. A member of the France squad at the 2006 World Cup.

TITUS BRAMBLE - 19

BORN	31 July 1981, Ipswich
POSITION	Centre Half
DEBUT	14 August 2002 v Zeljeznicar (A)
PREVIOUS CLUBS	Ipswich, Colchester

Titus is a powerful centre-half who joined United from Ipswich in July 2002. He began as a trainee at Ipswich, making his league debut in December 1998, when only 17. In 2000/01 he helped Town to a fifth place finish in the Premiership. The following season saw Ipswich slip out of the Premiership but a move to Tyneside rejuvenated his career. Titus was also an Under-21 international and his goal against Chelsea on the last day of the 2005/06 season confirmed United's 7th place finish and a place in the 2006/07 Intertoto Cup.

NICKY BUTT - 22

BORN	21 January 1975, Manchester
POSITION	Midfield
DEBUT	14 August 2004 v Middlesbrough (A)
PREVIOUS CLUBS	Manchester Utd, Birmingham (loan)

Nicky, a gritty, tigerish, but skillful ball winning midfielder who blends some tough tackling with good distribution, joined Newcastle from Manchester United in July 2004. After one season on Tyneside, he spent the 2005/06 campaign at Birmingham City but is now back on Tyneside. At Manchester United Nicky won six Premiership titles, two FA Cup winners medals and the European Champions League. The holder of 39 England caps, Nicky aims to make an impact at St. James' Park this season.

STEPHEN CARR - 2

BORN	29 August 1976, Dublin
POSITION	Right Back
DEBUT	14 August 2004 v Middlesbrough
PREVIOUS CLUB	Tottenham

Dublin born Stephen joined United in August 2004 from Tottenham Hotspur. He began life as a midfielder before joining Spurs as a YTS trainee in 1992. Stephen is an adventurous attack minded right back, but one very much aware of his defensive duties. A League Cup win with Tottenham in 1999 is his only major honour in the game but he was voted proudly in to the PFA Premiership team of the season in 2002/03. Back firing on all cylinders, Stephen has over 270 Premiership appearances under his belt, including eight goals.

KIERON DYER - 8

BORN	29 December 1978, Ipswich
POSITION	Midfield
DEBUT	7 August 1999 v Aston Villa (H)
PREVIOUS CLUB	Ipswich Town

Kieron was one of England's brightest young stars when he joined United from Ipswich in July 1999 and quickly demonstrated the talent which made him such hot property. Only 20 when he joined United, Kieron quickly added full England caps to the collection of Youth, U21 and B caps he had built up at Ipswich. Deceptively slim, Kieron has a strength in his balance which makes him hard to shake off the ball. Injuries have hampered his career at United as a fully fit Kieron is a constant danger to defences.

SHAY GIVEN - 1

BORN	20 April 1976, Lifford, Co. Donegal
POSITION	Goalkeeper
DEBUT	9 August 1997 v Sheffield Wednesday (H)
PREVIOUS CLUBS	Blackburn, Swindon, Sunderland

Republic of Ireland international who is now considered as the best in the Premiership. Since 2001 Shay has missed only two Premiership matches for United. He became United's most capped International player on 30 April 2003 when he won his 41st cap whilst at St. James' Park. Named Sports Personality of the Year by Sport Newcastle in March 2006, he made his 400th career appearance at Middlesbrough in April 2006 and captained United for the last 3 games of the season. Named in the Premiership team of the year for 2005/06.

STEVE HARPER - 12

BORN	14 March 1975, Easington
POSITION	Goalkeeper
DEBUT	28 November 1998 v Wimbledon (H)
PREVIOUS CLUBS	Bradford City (loan), Hartlepool (loan), Huddersfield (loan)

Steve signed for United from non-league football in 1993 but took six years to break into the first team and then played in the 1999 FA Cup Final against Manchester United in his 10th senior match! Before making his first-team debut, Steve went out on loan to Bradford City, Hartlepool and Huddersfield but has had to be patient in recent seasons as Shay Given took on the mantle as first choice goalkeeper in 2001. However, when Steve did play, he turned in excellent displays each time.

ALBERT LUQUE - 7

BORN	11 March 1978, Terrasso, Barcelona
POSITION	Striker
DEBUT	28 August 2005 v Man Utd (H)
PREVIOUS CLUB	Real Mallorca, Malaga, Deportivo (2002-05)

A Catalan by birth, Albert joined Barca as a youth player, moving on to Real Mallorca and then Malaga. It was there his career took off, 23 appearances and five goals were a good return for the 21 year old and he ended the season playing for Spain in the 2000 Olympic Games. Following the 2002 World Cup, Albert moved to Deportivo La Coruna and scored 12 La Liga goals in the 2002/03 campaign. After an injury-hit start to his United career, he scored the fourth goal in the derby victory at Sunderland in April.

JAMES MILNER - 16

BORN 4 January 1986, Leeds
POSITION Midfield/Winger
DEBUT 14 August 2004 v Middlesbrough
PREVIOUS CLUBS Swindon (loan), Leeds, Aston Villa (loan)

James, Leeds born and bred, is a very promising left sided midfielder cum winger. James was fast-tracked into the Leeds first team squad and in November 2002 became the second-youngest player to play in the Premiership. He went on to break Wayne Rooney's record as the youngest ever Premiership scorer by four days, aged just 16 and 357 days when he netted at Sunderland in December 2002. After making 40 appearances for the Magpies throughout 2004/05, he enjoyed a successful loan spell at Aston Villa last season.

CRAIG MOORE - 18

BORN 12 December 1975, Canterbury, Australia
POSITION Centre half
DEBUT 22 March 2006 v Chelsea (FAC) (A)
PREVIOUS CLUBS Australian Inst of Sport, Glasgow Rangers, C Palace, B. Moenchengladbach

Craig Moore began his career with the Australian Institute of Sport before joining the Glasgow Rangers youth set-up when he was 17. After five seasons at Ibrox, Moore moved to Crystal Palace for a short spell before returning to Glasgow. Strong in the tackle, and with good aerial ability, Craig at his best is a formidable defender. He joined The Magpies for the 2005/06 season and after a run of injuries, impressed during the successful run United enjoyed at the end of the season. Played and scored in the 2006 World Cup.

CHARLES N'ZOGBIA - 14

BORN 28 May 1986, Harfleur, France
POSITION Midfield
DEBUT 11 September 2004 v Blackburn (H)
PREVIOUS CLUBS La Havre

N'Zogbia signed for United in 2004 after FIFA's Players' Status Department confirmed to Newcastle United his right to an international transfer from Le Havre, the French Second Division Club. Charles was rated as one of the brightest prospects in France and he is on his way to fulfilling his potential on Tyneside after cementing himself a place in the first team during the last six weeks of the 2004/05 season. Blossomed last season with some exhilarating play and has much to look forward to in 2006/07.

MICHAEL OWEN - 10

BORN 14 December 1979, Chester
POSITION Striker
DEBUT 10 September 2005 v Fulham (H)
PREVIOUS CLUBS Liverpool, Real Madrid

Michael Owen is a world-class player with just under a goal every two games in international football - his combination of skill, pace and ability to read the game making him a unique talent. He is fourth in the all-time England hotshots list with his memorable goal against Argentina in the 1998 World Cup being voted as the Goal of the Tournament. A broken metatarsal bone in his foot in December 2005, and his cruciate knee injury during the World Cup were devastating blows for the player and Newcastle United.

SCOTT PARKER - 17

BORN 13 October 1980, Lambeth, London
POSITION Midfield
DEBUT 3 August 2005 v Deportivo (H)
PREVIOUS CLUBS Charlton, Norwich (loan), Chelsea

Scott joined United in June 2005 from Premiership Champions Chelsea, having previously been with London rivals Charlton Athletic. A very self-assured player, he has good vision, excellent distribution and a tremendous work-rate to match. Parker has represented England at every level from U15 to senior and now is firmly established as one of the fans' favourites at Newcastle. He scored his first United goal at Cheltenham in the FA Cup but a bout of glandular fever in March 2006 brought his 2005/06 campaign to a premature close.

MATTHEW PATTISON - 35

BORN 27 October 1986, Johannesburg, South Africa
POSITION Midfield
DEBUT 25 February 2006 v Everton (H)
PREVIOUS CLUB Academy

Born in South Africa, Matty moved to England with his family when he was 11 and joined the United Academy when he was 14. A stocky and aggressive midfielder, he had already established a good goals per game ratio at United before playing in a first team friendly at Celtic in August 2004. Matty made his first team bow as a substitute versus Everton on 25 February 2006 and performed very creditably. Awarded the 'Wor Jackie' award by Sport Newcastle on 13 March 2006.

PETER RAMAGE - 26

BORN 22 November 1983, Ashington
POSITION Defender
DEBUT 16 March 2005 v Olympiacos (H)
PREVIOUS CLUB Academy

Captain of the successful Under 17 Academy team during the 2000/01 season, Peter is a whole-hearted player who has grabbed his chance with both hands. Peter won the 'Wor Jackie' award from Sport Newcastle in March 2003 and made his first team debut against Olympiacos at St. James' Park in March 2005, following that up with his first Premiership match at Old Trafford in April 2005. Versatile and dependable across the back four, Peter is aiming to continue his progress at United during 2006/07.

NOBBY SOLANO - 4

BORN 12 December 1974 in Callao, Peru
POSITION Winger
DEBUT 22 August 1998 v Chelsea (A)
PREVIOUS CLUBS Sporting Crystal, Boca Juniors, Aston Villa

Nobby rejoined United in August 2005 having left the Magpies in January 2004 for Aston Villa. Solano became the first Peruvian to play in England when he came to Newcastle via Boca Juniors of Argentina in August 1998. A slight but skilful ball-player, Nobby is a dead-ball expert and first class crosser who creates many chances from wide positions. Nobby enjoyed a sparkling 2005/06 campaign, scoring some outstanding goals and amongst the current squad he is United's leading goalscorer with 44 goals.

STEVEN TAYLOR - 27

BORN 23 January 1986, Greenwich, London
POSITION Centre Half
DEBUT 25 March 2004 v Real Mallorca (A)
PREVIOUS CLUBS Wycombe (loan)

Steven, a dominating and mature centre-half, was honoured with the captaincy of the England Under 16 and 17 teams as he first began to make a name for himself in the game. He spent one month on loan at Wycombe in December 2003 before making his United first team debut on 25 March 2004 against Real Mallorca, following that up by making his first appearance in the Premiership three days later at Bolton Wanderers. A dislocated shoulder wrecked his 2005/06 campaign after a promising start to the season.

SUMMER SIGNING

DAMIEN DUFF - 11

BORN	2 March 1979, Ballyboden
POSITION	Winger
DEBUT	10 August 2006 v FK Ventspils (A)
PREVIOUS CLUBS	Blackburn, Chelsea

Damien Duff joined Newcastle United on 22 July 2006 from Premiership Champions Chelsea. Damien was signed by Blackburn as a trainee from Dublin side Lourdes Celtic when he was 17 and stayed with the club for seven years before moving to Chelsea where he won two Premiership titles. Duff is now one of the most feared wingers in Europe with pace, accurate crossing and impressive finishing combined with great versatility. Duff joins the Magpies at the peak of his career and intends spending the next few seasons helping United to success on both domestic and European fronts.

MANAGERIAL STAFF

GLENN ROEDER

Glenn Roeder was formally unveiled as Newcastle United's new manager on 16 May 2006, having taken over the reigns as Caretaker Manager on 2 February 2006. Having been working as Academy Manager since the start of the 2005/06 season, Roeder transformed the fortunes of the Magpies, guiding them to 11 wins and 2 draws in his 17 games in charge – an astonishing achievement given United's mid season predicament.

Glenn was born in Essex on 13 December 1955 and first played at Leyton Orient and Queens Park Rangers before moving to Newcastle United in 1984 where he helped the Magpies to promotion to the top-flight in a super side containing the likes of Keegan, Waddle and Beardsley.

After retiring in 1992, Glenn turned his hand to coaching which included a significant spell with West Ham and notably, with England at the 1998 World Cup where he assisted Glenn Hoddle. In 2005 Glenn returned to the North East to take charge of United's Academy, and the rest as they say is history!

KEVIN BOND

Kevin Bond's career began at Bournemouth in the early 1970s. Kevin, primarily a full back, then moved to Norwich and after a spell with Seattle Sounders in the NASL, Bond returned to English football in 1981 when he linked up with Manchester City, before moving on to Southampton and finally finishing his league career back at Bournemouth.

After a spell as Manager at Stafford Rangers in October 1997, Kevin teamed up with Alan Ball at Portsmouth, coached at West Ham, then joined forces with Harry Redknapp at Portsmouth before he made the switch to Southampton in December 2004.

When Redknapp returned to Fratton Park, once again Bond remained by his side before being tempted by Roeder to make the move to Tyneside in as Assistant Manager in June 2006.

TOMMY CRAIG

Tommy was the most expensive teenager on record when he moved from Aberdeen to Sheffield Wednesday in May 1969 for £100,000. The Hillsborough outfit hit bad times though and Craig's undoubted talent was revitalised when he moved to Tyneside. Possessing a terrific left foot, Tommy was a stylish and classy midfielder and gained his only Scotland cap whilst at St. James' Park.

Tommy left United for Aston Villa in 1978 and later went on to play for Swansea City and Carlisle United before turning to coaching. In July 1982, Tommy became assistant Manager at Carlisle United, moved to Hibernian as player-coach in October 1984, and then joined his boyhood heroes Celtic in 1987 where he held various roles at Parkhead.

Kenny Dalglish brought Tommy to Newcastle United in April 1998 to fulfil the role of Reserve Team Coach, a position he has ably held since then as well as being a highly respected SFA Coach.

LEE CLARK

Lee made his United debut back in the 1990/91 season alongside the likes of other local boys Robbie Elliott, Steve Watson and Alan Thompson. He teamed up well with Andy Cole as United were tagged the 'Entertainers' before he made the switch to Sunderland in 1997 before moving to Craven Cottage in the 1999/2000 season. And after six seasons with Fulham, Clark's career turned full circle following his move back to Gallowgate where he made many telling contributions to the side during the 2005/06 season.

In the summer of 2006, following the appointment of Glenn Roeder, Lee was offered a coaching position at St. James' Park, a role he gleefully accepted although he has retained his playing registration.

And as well as the aforementioned staff, there are many others who contribute hugely to the successful running of the Club: Scout David Mills, Terry McDermott who holds coaching and scouting duties, Doctor Roddy Macdonald, Physio Derek Wright, Fitness Coach Paul Winsper, Goalkeeping Coach Terry Gennoe plus a number of other medical and back up staff.

WORDSEARCH

See if you can find the 15 words associated with Newcastle United in the wordsearch below -

S	B	R	U	P	V	R	V	R	S	O	W	E	N	B	E	N
T	L	E	R	P	X	W	O	B	M	P	Q	A	U	G	R	E
J	X	T	V	A	C	A	D	E	M	Y	Y	R	M	M	Y	W
A	T	V	P	T	W	Q	H	K	D	U	T	E	B	U	I	C
M	R	O	A	P	O	M	W	Q	E	E	C	T	E	Y	K	A
E	A	Z	O	Q	A	F	S	H	E	A	R	E	R	R	P	S
S	I	D	W	N	S	N	I	R	G	Q	K	F	N	Q	V	T
P	N	S	B	L	A	C	K	A	N	D	W	H	I	T	E	L
A	I	X	Q	E	R	R	O	P	W	Y	R	T	N	L	P	E
R	N	A	D	E	R	Q	M	S	V	S	Y	H	E	W	G	U
K	G	U	L	M	Q	M	I	Y	F	W	G	J	Y	T	U	P
D	G	W	Y	A	C	X	M	A	J	K	E	I	V	L	J	O
T	R	E	L	G	A	D	I	D	A	S	O	W	V	T	M	N
E	O	T	C	P	J	Q	T	K	L	N	R	X	U	E	R	T
U	U	H	M	I	L	B	U	R	N	A	D	I	E	Q	N	Y
K	N	G	Z	E	A	D	W	Q	L	S	I	C	B	F	Y	N
B	D	D	Q	S	X	H	G	T	M	K	E	R	Y	X	W	E

ST JAMES PARK
SHEARER
MAGPIES
TOONARMY
NUMBER NINE
NEWCASTLE UPON TYNE
GEORDIE
BLACK AND WHITE
MILBURN
OWEN
ROEDER
ACADEMY
TRAINING GROUND
ADIDAS
GIVEN

Answers on page 61

NAME THAT FACE

Answers on page 61

JUNIOR MAGPIES

Why not show your true colours and join the only Official NUFC young supporters club – Junior Magpies??

'Official Sponsors of Junior Magpies'

As a young supporter you can become a member of Junior Magpies. We aim to enhance your support by providing exclusive members' benefits, bringing you closer to the heart of Newcastle United.

This year's membership includes:

An exclusive Membership Pack on joining, featuring:

Fab Mini Football,

Awesome Autograph book,

Cool Bootbag,

Plus – your personalised Membership Card and Certificate

All supplied in Junior Magpies Presentation Box

TOP TEN GOALS 2005/06

We saw some cracking goals during the 2005/06 campaign, some rip roaring strikes, some the end result of great build up play, others were flashes of individual brilliance.

CHARLES N'ZOGBIA V BLACKBURN (A), 18/9/05

United were cruising when Celestine Babayaro played a fine forward ball down the left flank to N'Zogbia. Homing in on goal, the young French ace adroitly rolled his foot over the top of the ball to bamboozle Brad Friedel leaving him the simple task of knocking the ball into the unguarded net. A sublime finish.

MICHAEL OWEN V MANCHESTER CITY (H), 24/9/05

The moment all of Tyneside were waiting for. After opening his United account at Blackburn the previous week, Lee Bowyer fed Owen who advanced into the penalty area to slide the ball past England colleague David James with one expert touch. Typically clinical.

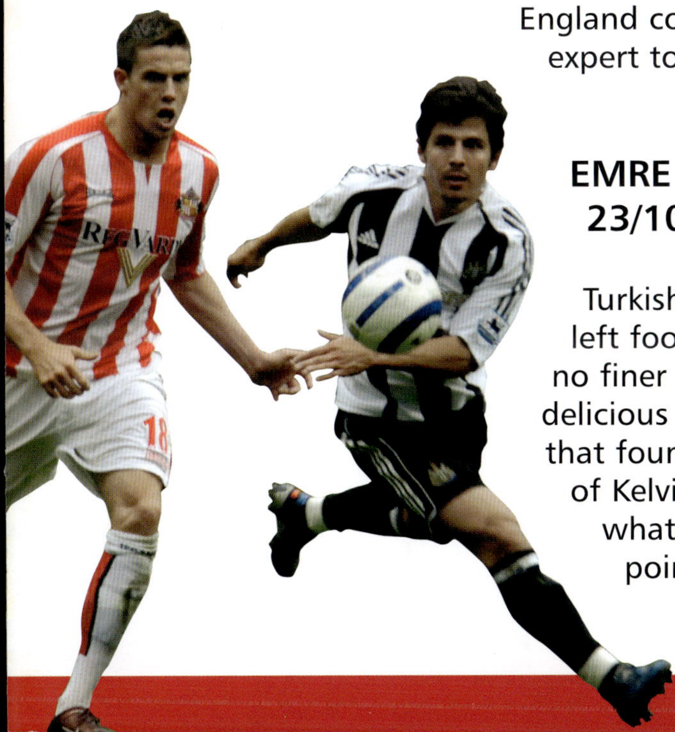

EMRE V SUNDERLAND (H), 23/10/05

Turkish international Emre has a sweet left foot and this was demonstrated in no finer fashion than when he curled a delicious shot round the Sunderland wall that found the back of the net courtesy of Kelvin Davis' right hand post – and what's more, it gave United the three points in the season's first derby encounter. Brilliant.

ALAN SHEARER V PORTSMOUTH (H), 4/2/06

The record breaking goal. The master headed on Shay Given's long goal kick and when strike partner Shola Ameobi played the ball back into his path, Shearer knocked the ball past the onrushing Dean Kiely from 10 yards. Shearer saluted his adoring public and the adulation for him boomed out from all four corners of the ground. Quite magnificent.

NOBBY SOLANO V EVERTON (H), 25/2/06

Already a goal to the good, scored by the Peruvian maestro, Lee Bowyer found Solano in space on the right hand edge of the penalty area. Instant control saw him cut inside and curl a fabulous shot with the outside of his right foot into the corner of the net past a helpless Sander Westerveld. Genius.

SCOTT PARKER V CHARLTON (A), 26/3/06

Parker returned to south London to play at The Valley for the first time since leaving the Addicks for Chelsea in January 2004. Yet to open his Premiership goalscoring account for United, Parker received the ball from Alan Shearer fully 30 yards from goal and let fly with a strike that flew past Thomas Myhre. His celebration was a joy to behold.

LEE BOWYER V TOTTENHAM (H), 1/4/06

A terrific team goal. Less than 2 minutes into the game, Shearer, Solano and N'Zogbia combined down the left and when the Frenchman delivers the ball into the area, Bowyer appears from nowhere, after a typically lung busting run, to beat Paul Robinson and send United on their way to a well deserved victory. Fantastic football.

NEWCASTLE UNITED

MICHAEL CHOPRA V SUNDERLAND (A), 17/4/06

This wasn't exactly a fantastic net buster, more a crucial strike. Titus Bramble plants a free kick into the Sunderland penalty area and substitute Chopra capitalises on a misunderstanding between Kelvin Davis and Steve Caldwell to triumphantly knock the ball into an empty net as pandemonium breaks out amongst the visiting fans behind the goal.

ALAN SHEARER V SUNDERLAND (A), 17/4/06

Shearer's 206th and last goal for United. Charles N'Zogbia is felled in the box and United's Number 9 buries the ball in the back of the net, his thumping strike giving Kelvin Davis no chance. A trademark celebration follows as he stands, arms aloft milking the applause from the Geordie hordes behind the goal. Priceless.

TITUS BRAMBLE V CHELSEA (H), 7/5/06

United knew they needed a goal to edge past Bolton into 7th place in the Premiership. With 17 minutes remaining of United's season, Emre swung across a corner at the Gallowgate End and when Amady Faye headed the ball back across goal, Titus Bramble was on hand to majestically volley the ball past Lenny Pidgeley. St. James' Park erupted.

HONOURS AND RECORDS

FOUNDED: as Newcastle East End 1882

FOOTBALL LEAGUE CHAMPIONS: 1905, 1907, 1909, 1927

FA PREMIER LEAGUE RUNNERS-UP: 1996, 1997

FL DIVISION ONE CHAMPIONS: 1993

FL DIVISION TWO CHAMPIONS: 1965

FA CUP WINNERS: 1910, 1924, 1932, 1951, 1952, 1955

FA CUP RUNNERS-UP: 1905, 1906, 1908, 1911, 1974, 1998, 1999

FL CUP RUNNERS-UP: 1976

FA CHARITY SHIELD WINNERS: 1909

FA CHARITY SHIELD RUNNERS-UP: 1933, 1952, 1953, 1956, 1996

INTER CITIES FAIRS CUP WINNERS: 1969

TEXACO CUP WINNERS: 1974, 1975

ANGLO ITALIAN CUP WINNERS: 1973

RECORD ATTENDANCE: 68,386 v Chelsea September 1930

RECORD VICTORY: 13-0 v Newport County (H) October 1946

RECORD DEFEAT: 0-9 v Burton WDS (A) April 1895

MOST LEAGUE & CUP GOALS IN A CAREER:
206 by Alan Shearer 1996-2006

MOST LEAGUE & CUP GOALS IN A SEASON: 41 by Andy Cole 1993-94

MOST LEAGUE & CUP APPEARANCES IN A CAREER:
496 by Jimmy Lawrence 1904-22

MOST CAPPED PLAYER:
Shay Given, 67 caps for Republic of Ireland, 1997 - 2006

YOUNGEST PLAYER:
Steve Watson, 16 years 223 days (November 1990 v Wolves)

OLDEST PLAYER:
William Hampson, 44 years 225 days (April 1927 v Birmingham)

RECORD TRANSFER FEE RECEIVED:
£13.65m from Real Madrid for Jonathan Woodgate (2004)

RECORD TRANSFER FEE PAID:
£16m to Real Madrid for Michael Owen (2005)

NEWCASTLE UNITED'S PREMIER LEAGUE RECORD 1993/94 – 2005/06

	PL	W	D	L	F	A	PTS	POS
1993/94	42	23	8	11	82	41	77	3rd
1994/95	42	20	12	10	67	47	72	6th
1995/96	38	24	6	8	66	37	78	2nd
1996/97	38	19	11	8	73	40	68	2nd
1997/98	38	11	11	16	35	44	44	13th
1998/99	38	11	13	14	48	54	46	13th
1999/00	38	14	10	14	63	54	52	11th
2000/01	38	14	9	15	44	50	51	11th
2001/02	38	21	8	9	74	52	71	4th
2002/03	38	21	6	11	63	48	69	3rd
2003/04	38	13	17	8	52	40	56	5th
2004/05	38	10	14	14	47	57	44	14th
2005/06	38	17	7	14	47	42	58	7th
	502	**218**	**132**	**152**	**761**	**606**	**786**	

ALL TIME PREMIER LEAGUE RECORDS (1992/93 – DATE)

		Pl	W	D	L	F	A	Pts
1	Manchester United	544	339	126	79	1057	486	1143
2	Arsenal	544	289	146	109	909	481	1013
3	Liverpool	544	265	136	143	868	552	931
4	Chelsea	544	261	147	136	848	556	930
5	**Newcastle United**	**502**	**218**	**132**	**152**	**761**	**606**	**786**
6	Aston Villa	544	202	159	183	668	632	765
7	Tottenham Hotspur	544	196	143	205	716	731	731
8	Blackburn Rovers	468	190	125	153	650	553	695
9	Leeds United	468	189	125	154	641	573	692
10	Everton	544	178	146	220	652	738	680

ACADEMY & RESERVES

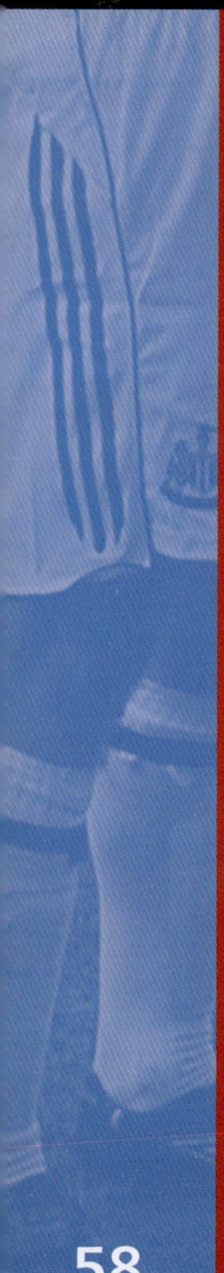

As well as the first team at Newcastle United, the Club also has Reserve and Under 18 teams, both of which are in place primarily to nurture potential future first team players.

The Reserves is like it sounds, a platform for young players who have generally come through the Academy system and are now taking the next step on the ladder to what they hope will be a successful career in football. It's not uncommon either for members of the first team squad to play for the Reserves on occasions throughout the season, which is usually the case if they're returning from an injury, or looking to build up their match fitness or form.

The Reserves squad enjoyed a pretty successful season in 2005/06. They play in the Barclays Reserve League Northern Division, which as the name suggests, is a division made up of the Reserve sides from United's fellow clubs in the Premiership. United finished fifth in the division last season and also achieved the distinction of being the only team in the country not to lose a home league game throughout the whole season.

The Newcastle United Reserve team also competes in the Northumberland Senior Cup, won last season by United who beat those renowned cup fighters Blyth Spartans 2 – 1 in the Final, Alan O'Brien scoring twice to clinch victory.

Coach to the Reserves is former United midfielder from the 1970s, Tommy Craig, who is also a respected Coach with the Scottish Football Association. He even helped Alan Shearer through his coaching course last summer!

The Newcastle United Football Academy has its own training venue and it really is a first class facility. Players join the Academy from as young as seven, training regularly in the evenings after school has finished and teams are run from the Under-9 age category right through to the Under 18s. It's that age group that competes in the FA Premier Academy League, playing matches throughout the season against teams from both the Premiership and the Championship/League One. Last season United finished third in the Northern Division of the Academy League but they also enjoyed a very successful run to the semi finals of the FA Youth Cup, before losing gallantly to Manchester City over two legs.

The Academy acts as a specialist development centre where talented young players are coached and trained. The Academy has highly qualified specialist coaches and support from other professional staff including doctors, physiotherapists and teachers. And it's not just about football, for the scholars who enter the Academy are provided with an all-round development and educational programme which is absolutely vital, especially to those who don't make the grade.

THE TRAINING GROUND

Newcastle United's training grounds, both for the first team and the academy, are among the very best in the country and feature the latest in modern technology to ensure the players get the most out of their training sessions.

Located just outside the city centre in Benton the training grounds, opened in 2003, feature 13 all-weather and two outdoor floodlit pitches across the two sites as well as a full size indoor hall. This allows the players to train in any weather without the risk of flooded or frost hardened pitches.

The indoor hall is truly huge measuring 96m x 68m and is the biggest of its kind in Europe. For the pitches, 144,000 tonnes of earth were moved and 14 miles of drains used to stop them becoming waterlogged.

Both venues also have gyms with state-of-the-art equipment, restaurants, changing facilities and relaxation areas where the players can watch TV or play snooker.

However not everyone who uses the training ground is a Newcastle United player. In the past the facilities have been used by the Newcastle Falcons rugby team and Ashes hero Steve Harmison who is an avid Magpies supporter.

As the academy is situated directly opposite the first team facility, young players get to see stars such as Michael Owen and Shay Given everyday and know that they could one day get the chance to be on the pitch with them!

QUIZ ANSWERS

QUIZ 1 (Page 19)

What do you remember about the 2005/06 season?

1. Charles N'Zogbia (v Fulham)
2. Deportivo La Coruna
3. Inter Milan
4. Manchester City
5. Mansfield
6. Jermaine Jenas
7. Lee Clark
8. Liverpool
9. Portsmouth
10. Tottenham

QUIZ 2 (Page 29)

See how much you know about Newcastle United past and present!

1. 7
2. Celtic
3. Matty Pattison
4. 1969
5. West Ham United
6. 1996/97
7. Shay Given
8. Nobby Solano
9. 6
10. 1993/4

WORDSEARCH

(Page 46)

S	B	R	U	P	V	R	V	R	S	O	W	E	N	B	E	N
T	L	E	R	P	X	W	O	B	M	P	Q	A	U	G	R	E
J	X	T	V	A	C	A	D	E	M	Y	Y	R	M	M	Y	W
A	T	V	P	T	W	Q	H	K	D	U	T	E	B	U	I	C
M	R	O	A	P	O	M	W	Q	E	E	C	T	E	Y	K	A
E	A	Z	O	Q	A	F	S	H	E	A	R	E	R	R	P	S
S	I	D	W	N	S	N	I	R	G	Q	K	F	N	Q	V	T
P	N	S	B	L	A	C	K	A	N	D	W	H	I	T	E	L
A	I	X	Q	E	R	R	O	P	W	Y	R	T	N	L	P	E
R	N	A	D	E	R	Q	M	S	V	S	Y	H	E	W	G	U
K	G	U	L	M	Q	M	I	Y	F	W	G	J	Y	T	U	P
D	G	W	Y	A	C	X	M	A	J	K	E	I	V	L	J	O
T	R	E	L	G	A	D	I	D	A	S	O	W	V	T	M	N
E	O	T	C	P	J	Q	T	K	L	N	R	X	U	E	R	T
U	U	H	M	I	L	B	U	R	N	A	D	I	E	Q	N	Y
K	N	G	Z	E	A	D	W	Q	L	S	I	C	B	F	Y	N
B	D	D	Q	S	X	H	G	T	M	K	E	R	Y	X	W	E

ST JAMES PARK
SHEARER
MAGPIES
TOONARMY
NUMBER NINE
NEWCASTLE UPON TYNE
GEORDIE
BLACK AND WHITE
MILBURN
OWEN
ROEDER
ACADEMY
TRAINING GROUND
ADIDAS
GIVEN

NAME THAT FACE

(Page 47)

1: EMRE
2: TAYLOR
3: BABAYARO

northern rock